SHIRE NATURAL H

D1461095

THE KINGFISHER

DAVID BOAG

CONTENTS

COVER: *The Common Kingfisher is one of Britain's most spectacular birds, both in its plumage and in its lifestyle.*

Series editors: Jim Flegg and Chris Humphries

Set in 9 point Times roman and printed in Great Britain by C. I. Thomas & Sons (Haverfordwest) Ltd, Press Buildings, Merlins Bridge, Haverfordwest, Dyfed.

The Kingfisher

The beautiful plumage of the Common Kingfisher serves as a reminder that this species is part of a family that is mainly tropical. There are about ninety different species of kingfisher in the world and these form the Alcedinidae family. All members of this family catch living prey but many of them do not rely upon water for their food supply. These species (often called forest kingfishers) may live many miles from water and feed on insects and reptiles. The Australian Kookaburra (*Alcedo* spp.) and the African Striped Kingfisher (*Halcyon chelicuti*), for example, have little interest in water, whereas the North American Belted Kingfisher (*Ceryle alcyon*) and the African Malachite Kingfisher (*Alcedo cristata*) both rely heavily on the rivers and lakes for their food supply. Their sources of food may be different but in shape and movement the family likeness can be recognised.

Size is variable, from tiny kingfishers only 12 centimetres (4¾ inches) long, to the huge Laughing Kookaburra (*Alcedo novaeguineae*) which is as large as a crow. They all nest in holes in trees, termite mounds or earth banks and many species construct their own nest holes. Although most kingfishers have distinctive calls, none could be described as having a song. There are many other shared characteristics and it is interesting to note the family affinity with the colour blue. On many species of kingfisher a brilliant, iridescent blue area is visible on the plumage, perhaps over the whole of the back or only on a wing bar. In only a few species, for example, the Pied Kingfisher (*Ceryle rudis*), is the blue completely absent. The Alcedinidae family is represented in all parts of the globe, with the exception of the polar regions, and it is the Common Kingfisher (*Alcedo atthis*) that is the most northerly and ranges furthest from the tropics.

The Common Kingfisher can be found throughout most of Europe, breeding from a northern limit of about mid Sweden south to North Africa. The European race (*Alcedo atthis ispida*) spreads east from Britain as far as the Caspian Sea and south to Spain, whilst other races cover the south-east of Europe, North Africa and most of Asia. It is remarkable that this species is equally at home beside a river bank in Britain, Africa, India or Japan. In Germany or Scotland they may need to move south as the ice of winter encroaches on their territory, while others will be sheltering from the equatorial sun.

In Britain the Kingfisher's range covers the whole of England, Wales and Ireland but in Scotland it is found only in the southern counties. Although the species may be found throughout its range, it becomes more thinly distributed in the north of the area and in Ireland, particularly in the west. Its range is limited not only by climatic conditions but also by suitable habitat. The Kingfisher's requirements are fairly flexible but it prefers slow-moving, lowland rivers, lakes and ponds, and cannot tolerate fast, tumbling mountain streams. Meandering rivers with plenty of shallows that contain shoals of minnows are ideal. Trees overhanging the water provide security and fishing perches, and a high vertical bank supplies the requirements for nesting. As with most birds, any location where a supply of food is available will become part of a Kingfisher's territory. Some Kingfishers will regularly visit garden ponds to steal goldfish.

British Kingfishers do not usually undertake long distance journeys except in conditions of extreme cold, when frozen rivers may drive the birds towards the coast. The vast majority of juveniles are able to establish a territory for themselves within ten miles of where they were raised. There are always exceptions to the rule and a few birds have been found dead on lightships and three or four ringed birds have been recovered which have crossed either to or from the continent. It would seem that continental birds more frequently travel long distances.

The legendary blue of the Kingfisher

1. *A riverbank typical of the kind that a pair of Kingfishers might choose as a nest site, excavating a tunnel into the vertical bank. Below ground the brood is safe from predators.*
2. *The same river, photographed a few days later when in flood. If flooding occurs during the breeding season many Kingfisher eggs may be lost or chicks drowned in their nests.*

eludes descriptions such as 'electric blue', 'azure blue', 'dazzling cobalt'. The blue/green is no single colour and will vary depending upon the quality and angle of the light shimmering on the plumage because it is the result of reflected and refracted light within the feather structure rather than a pigment. The brightest iridescent blue strip runs down the Kingfisher's back to the tip of its tail. The bird's wings and head are coloured a darker shade of the same blue and many of the contour feathers have a brighter spot at the tip. The bright spots form dotted lines on the wings and a speckled pattern on the head. In contrast, the underparts are a warm chestnut-orange: these include the breast, flanks, belly and underside of the tail. A patch of the chestnut orange is situated below and behind the bird's eye. The chin and throat are white and the plumage is completed by a white flash on the side of the neck. The short legs and feet of a mature bird are sealing-wax red, tipped with black claws. However, the young birds leave the nest with black feet and it is not until the juveniles are a couple of months old that the feet begin to change to red. Juveniles also show a white tip to the end of the beak for several months. The beak of the adult Kingfisher is the key to sexing the birds. The male has a glossy, black beak whilst the lower mandible of the female is coloured bright orange/red. It is not possible to sex them until they have begun to mature. As the feet change colour the females begin to develop the red pigment at the base of the lower mandible. The redness spreads along the mandible until at least half, and in some cases the whole, of the lower mandible is coloured. By the age of four or five months the juvenile birds will have almost fully developed colouration and will be adult size.

The Kingfisher is much smaller than is often imagined; it measures on average about 17.5 centimetres (6¾ inches) long, a fraction larger than a sparrow but certainly not as large as a starling. It often appears as a rather dumpy, compact bird with a chopped, short tail. Sitting on a branch in its characteristic upright stance, the Kingfisher often bobs its head and flicks its tail. Its long, sword-like beak will measure, on average, 4 centimetres (1½ inches) in length and the bird's lively black eyes are perfectly aligned with the beak, providing maximum sighting accuracy when diving for fish.

The flight of the Kingfisher is very direct and powerful, giving the impression of great speed. In normal flight it flies low over the water, flying purposefully as if it always knows exactly where it is going. The size and shape of the wings cause it to fly with a rapid, beating motion and the Kingfisher rarely glides, except in courtship. Even when manoeuvring in the air or preparing to land, the Kingfisher continues to beat its wings at full speed. It is able to use even the lightest breeze to hover in mid air, looking like a blue blur hanging over the water. The Common Kingfisher does not appear to hover from preference: it only uses that method to observe the water when suitable fishing branches are not available. If necessary it may hold the same position over the water for fifteen seconds or more. Other species of kingfisher, for example the Pied Kingfisher (*Ceryle rudis*), commonly hover for long periods and seems to prefer that method of looking for fish.

Whilst flying, the Kingfisher often utters its penetrating call, which carries effectively across the water. The call is best described as a high-pitched whistle, 'chee-chee', often used two or three times in succession. A variety of other sounds or calls have been attributed to the Kingfisher, including an attractive song, but the evidence to support this is very slim. The whistle is used in a variety of ways, depending on the situation. It may be used softly in the early spring months as a courtship or contact note between the male and female. Sitting only a few feet apart, they may whistle softly to each other in alternating cheeps, first one bird, then the other. During a territorial dispute the note becomes harder and is clipped short and sounds quite definitely aggressive. However, for most of the year the call is used to declare ownership of the river and it is commonly used in flight or immediately on landing.

4

3. *Looking down its long beak, the Kingfisher searches for its next meal.*

Territorial aggression

Ownership of a feeding territory is very important to a Kingfisher in Britain. It reserves the exclusive right to feed within that area and will attempt to chase off all other Kingfishers that dare to challenge its ownership. Generally territories are established in the late summer and autumn, although the winter territory may not contain a suitable nest location and as a result a proportion of the birds will need to move in the early spring. For example, some Kingfishers, particularly juvenile birds, will winter on estuaries and natural harbours and move to fresh water to breed.

The size of each individual's territory varies according to a variety of factors including the availability of fish, competition from other Kingfishers and the bird's ability to patrol the area effectively. In most areas of Britain the population of Kingfishers is not sufficiently high for competition to be a problem. It would seem, therefore, that the bird defends an area that includes a variety of good fishing locations. The outlying parts of the territory are less well defended because the birds cannot be on constant patrol. Most territories include about a mile of river but a nearby lake or ditch which also provides good fishing will be included. In some areas of southern

4. *African Pied Kingfishers are commonly seen hovering and do not display the characteristic 'kingfisher blue'.*

6

Europe, where the population is higher, territories may be considerably smaller. It is only during the breeding season that the male and female share the same stretch of river. Once the season is over their territorial instincts override all else, and after only a week or two of a rather irritable relationship the pair separate to live a solitary life for the rest of the year (which dispels the myth that Kingfishers pair for life).

A juvenile bird establishing its first territory arrives at a new location in silence. It has been chased from the parents' river, probably aggressively, and appears to be rather nervous. By remaining silent it is able to avoid detection for an hour or two whilst it steals a few fish. If left unchallenged, a few tentative calls demonstrate the bird's growing confidence. After only a few days of uninterrupted fishing the young Kingfisher regards the river as its own and will call with defiant confidence. From this stage the bird will be prepared to defend the territory if another Kingfisher arrives.

A dominant, powerful whistle is the first method of defending a territory, but if a newcomer is confident enough to stand its ground then a display battle will ensue. The birds will perch about a yard apart and display to each other in a silent ritual. At first the display takes the form of a very upright posture, with shoulders slightly hunched and beak held just open. The opponent positions itself to show the profile of its head to the best advantage, which presumably displays the size and power of the beak to most effect. For many minutes the adversaries will display in this way, standing like statues, staring each other out. There is no movement and no calling as the tension builds up between the two birds. If this display has no effect they then begin slowly to sway their heads, dipping down in a reptilian motion. It is an eerie display to observe. Eventually they dip low in silent aggression, with beaks still held open as they continue to display their profiles. These displays may go on for several hours between adversaries that are well matched in nerves. At some stage the weaker of the two will attempt to retreat and will be chased by the dominant bird, who now calls in angry defiance.

On very rare occasions adversaries may be equally determined to hold on to the territory and this will lead to physical combat. One bird will fly at the other whilst the defending bird gapes viciously in its direction. The pair may stab, peck and wrestle, using their beaks, until one is dislodged from the branch and may even fall into the water. This extreme aggressive behaviour is very rare, and in the majority of disputes the display deals with the situation. Certainly a Kingfisher will make a violent physical attack on a stuffed Kingfisher placed near a favourite fishing spot.

Although it is not likely that Kingfishers will actually kill each other, the display battle may continue for many hours. Valuable fishing time is lost during short winter days and a lot of nervous energy is expended in the process. Both birds are tired and hungry and the defeated bird may have to find fish in a strange part of the river. For the successful bird, however, the effort must be worthwhile because it gains the advantage of productive feeding locations in a river it knows well.

5. *With its wings beating the Kingfisher flies towards the water in pursuit of its prey.*

6. *As the bird enters the water its beak is opened and its eyes are closed.*

7. *Beneath the water the Kingfisher grabs for the fish.*

8. *Holding the fish firmly in its beak, the Kingfisher brings it to the surface.*

Feeding

As its name suggests, the Kingfisher's staple diet is fish, although other prey will be taken on occasions, including insects and amphibians. Dragonflies and dragonfly larvae, crayfish, newts, small frogs and so on may be included in the Kingfisher's diet and these will be taken from the water in the same way as fish. Continental birds appear to supplement their diet with insects and amphibians more readily than do British Kingfishers. In the author's experience British Kingfishers have a strong preference for fish and most birds prey exclusively on them throughout their lives.

The choice of species of fish is limited mainly by availability. Minnows swarm in the shallow water of many rivers and often there are shoals of small chub or roach in a lake. Any trout farmer will be familiar with the regular visits of the resident Kingfisher to the trout hatchery to feed on the fry, to such an extent that he needs to cover them with netting. All sources of fish are fair game to the Kingfisher and although some species may be preferred there appears to be no fish that the Kingfisher will reject. Size of fish is, of course, a limiting factor but they can cope with surprisingly large prey. Providing it is not a deep-bodied species, the Kingfisher can swallow a fish up to 8 centimetres (3¼ inches) long, that is, equal to half the bird's own body length. At times it seems impossible for the bird to accommodate such a large item of prey but it is rare for a Kingfisher to catch a fish too large for it to swallow. All items of prey are swallowed whole, and usually head first to prevent the fins or scales lodging in the bird's throat. The most accurate figures available suggest that about seventeen or eighteen minnows are eaten by an adult each day. This amounts to approximately 45 grams (3¼ ounces) equalling 1.2 times the bird's own body weight.

The Kingfisher has an intimate knowledge of its territory and the most productive fishing locations. If a selected site does not produce a meal the Kingfisher will not wait long before it leaves for a more likely area. Bearing in mind the speed of its flight, low over the water, and the constantly reflecting and rippling nature of the river, the bird's ability to spot fish is remarkable.

Once the Kingfisher has located a shoal of fish it may spend a few moments preparing to dive. It does not merely dive hopefully into the middle of the shoal: it aims for a particular fish, probably the largest and fattest if it is a shoal of minnows. Having selected the prey and waited for it to move into a catchable position, the Kingfisher launches itself towards the water. It does not merely drop or glide into the water but flies at the fish with beating wings. At the moment of impact the wings are folded over its back to effect a streamlined entry and the nictitating membrane (inner eyelid) is drawn across the eye. All the aspects of the dive have been calculated before the bird hits the water: it has judged the depth, taken into account the angle of refraction on the surface of the water, and allowed for the movement of the river and the fish. Once underwater it simply opens its beak and grabs at the position where it has calculated the fish to be. A Kingfisher does not deliberately spear a fish, it aims to grab it between the mandibles. If by accident a fish becomes impaled on a mandible the bird has a difficult task to remove it without dropping it back into the water. A Kingfisher may misjudge the dive and pick up a stone or twig from the river bed, but usually these items are dropped before the bird clears the water.

Understandably, the dive is extremely fast. In less than a second from leaving the branch, the fish is grabbed and held aloft as the Kingfisher flies out of the water. The bird returns to the surface mainly through its own buoyancy but a little wing flapping helps to boost the take-off from the water with a powerful downstroke. A great deal of effort is required for the Kingfisher to blast itself free of the surface tension of the water. It is important that the bird gets in and out of the water quickly, otherwise its feathers become waterlogged. Young Kingfishers find this difficult to do and may become wet and chilled and as a result many die.

Most dives for fish are from branches only 0.9 to 1.2 metres (3 to 4 feet) above the water. However, Kingfishers are able to dive from a hovering position or from a perch several feet up, checking themselves in mid-dive to align finally with the fish. Most fish are taken within the top 15 centimetres (6 inches) of water but deeper dives of 30 to 35 centimetres (12 to 14 inches) are possible. There is no doubt that Kingfishers prefer to catch fish in shallow water. In water only an inch or two deep the bird seizes a fish on almost every dive but in deeper water the success rate falls. In very shallow water the Kingfisher modifies its dive at the last moment so that it does not crash into the river bed: as soon as the beak enters the water, instead of folding its wings, it opens them and takes the impact of the water on its chest and wings to prevent too deep a dive.

PREENING

Like all species of birds Kingfishers need to keep their feathers in good condition, for feathers are not only essential for flight but also provide vital insulation.

Preening keeps the feathers clean and distributes oil from the preen gland. The Kingfisher nibbles each feather into place and zips them together to ensure an efficient wing surface for flight. Dirty feathers do not insulate the bird's body so well and cleanliness as well as oil is essential to waterproof the feathers. Sitting on a favourite, secluded branch the Kingfisher may spend over fifteen minutes thoroughly preening every part of its anatomy. Sometimes it may plunge into the water and then return to the branch to continue with its vigorous preening session, so presumably water helps preening. Feathers of the head and nape are scratched into place with the foot. A bird may spend several hours each day taking care of its feathers.

In the evening the Kingfisher finds a safe and secluded spot in which to spend the hours of darkness. Generally it is an area of dense cover, either an ivy-covered tree or a bush with thick foliage. A favourite roosting perch will be used for several months and as a result the location becomes marked by the bird's white excrement.

9. *The Kingfisher emerges from the water with the fish, expending a great deal of effort in getting clear.*

10. *The Striped King-fisher of Africa is not associated with water and feeds mainly on insects and small reptiles.*

11. *An African king-fisher that is closely related to the European species is the Malachite Kingfisher.*

Breeding

COURTSHIP

In Britain the breeding season begins early in the year. Some pairs may form as early as mid February while others may not meet until the end of March. Having spent the preceding months aggressively defending a territory, it is hardly surprising that confusion arises when the male and female first meet. It is not uncommon for the same pair of birds to meet again after spending the winter apart, but this is by no means the rule.

At first they are unsure of each other, displaying more in aggression than courtship. It is at this time of year that courtship flight takes place. Instead of flying low over the water, following every twist and turn of the river, the pair fly high, above the tree tops. Often there is a lot of excited calling as they chase each other high over the river. Should winter weather conditions suddenly return, the pair will separate again until brighter conditions encourage them to reunite.

The urge for the male to courtship feed the female is very strong, even from their first meeting. The male will dive into the water and return to the branch with a quivering fish. Having stunned the fish on the branch, it will then turn it to face head outwards. The male flies to the female and edges towards her, reaching out to offer the fish he has prepared for her. With much excited calling, the fish is taken by the female and swallowed. Courtship feeding continues until the end of incubation and will resume at the start of a second brood. The pair rapidly become accustomed to each other and the female will expect to be fed by the male, persuading him with begging, quivering wings. The act of courtship feeding strengthens a pair bond between the birds and assists the female to build up body condition for egg laying.

Also associated with courtship is a display posture that is used mainly by the male. The bird stands very upright, giving the impression of being tall and slim. The tail is held down and the wings are also drooped forward and down so that the primary feathers almost cover the feet. The head and neck are held stiff and angular, as the beak is tilted at a slight upwards angle. As in the aggressive display, the aim is to show the bird's profile to the best advantage, but in courtship the beak is held closed.

Excited whistles often accompany courtship activity, but on occasions the pair may sit a couple of feet apart and call to each other with soft, alternating cheeps. Although this can be connected with courtship it is also a contact call between the pair, helping to strengthen the pair bond that must last through the breeding season.

NEST CONSTRUCTION

Even during the earliest stages of courtship the pair of Kingfishers will show interest in a nest site. Kingfishers nest underground in a chamber at the end of a tunnel all of which they construct themselves. A suitable nest bank will vary from one area to another, depending on availability, but it is ideally a vertical wall of soft clay soil directly above the river. In some localities, where ideal nest banks are not available, some pairs may be forced to nest a short distance from the river and others may make use of less suitable soil. However, all nest tunnels are dug into vertical banks and are usually within the top 90 centimetres (3 feet), no matter how high the bank.

At first the pair fly at the soil all over the bank and peck at it before falling backwards. Eventually they concentrate their efforts on one spot where they are able to make a depression and then, taking it in turns, they tunnel in. The tunnel is dug at a slight upwards angle which allows for drainage. This is most important as the young Kingfishers develop in the nest. Unless an obstruction such as a rock or large root causes the Kingfishers to deviate, the tunnel is straight. This permits a little light to enter the chamber and this source of light is very important for the orderly running of the nest. The young Kingfishers squirt their rather liquid excreta towards the light and therefore down the tunnel. They also sit facing the tunnel waiting in the gloom for the adult to bring a fish. Most tunnels are 60 to 90 centimetres (2 to 3 feet) long before the chamber is hollowed out at the end. To dig the tunnel the birds peck at the soil to loosen it, violently pulling and twisting at any roots that obstruct the way. The loose soil is then scraped backwards by the feet, until a small pile of soil collects behind the bird. The diameter of the tunnel does not allow the birds to turn around and as they reverse out the feet continue to kick the soil backwards. The tail also pushes the loose earth down the tunnel, out of the end and into the water.

Kingfishers always keep watch over each other while the digging is in progress. While one of the pair is in the nest digging, the other waits outside, watching the trickle of soil falling from the entrance. When the digging bird leaves the work, with soil-covered beak, it is immediately replaced by the other. At any sign of danger the guarding bird will utter its powerful whistle as it leaves the nest bank and the other Kingfisher will heed the warning and follow it up river. Depending on the time of year and the weather conditions, it may take little more than a week or well over a month to complete the tunnel. It would seem that pairs of Kingfishers beginning construction very early in the season do not have the same sense of urgency and spend less time each day digging. They are also deterred from digging by adverse weather conditions. As a result the early workers make slower progress than the late beginners and most chambers are completed about late March or early April.

It is usual for Kingfishers to dig a new nest chamber each year. They may even use another bank, although there appears to be a strong attraction to certain banks which may be used for many years. Therefore many generations of Kingfishers will dig tunnels into the bank and the evidence of this can be seen by the remains of old tunnels. Within one season it is common for them to have a second or even a third brood in the same chamber. However, this is only a generalisation because while on odd occasions

Kingfishers use a tunnel for several years they also occasionally dig a new tunnel for a second brood.

Once the chamber is complete at the end of the tunnel the birds are able to turn around in the chamber and come out forwards. This is a good indication that egg laying will begin shortly. Copulation will take place at this time. Kingfishers may copulate two or three times each day, for about a week, around the egg laying period. The first egg is laid on the bare soil of the hollowed-out chamber. There is no attempt to line the nest, although during incubation a collection of fish bones and scales cover the floor because the incubating bird regurgitates pellets in the nest.

The eggs are pure white; they do not need to be camouflaged in the security of the underground nest chamber. An egg is laid each day, usually each morning, until the clutch is completed. The most common clutch size is seven, although six is only slightly less common. Clutch sizes ranging from four to ten eggs have been recorded but these are comparatively rare. Most first clutches are laid during the first two weeks of April, although the precise timing will vary depending on weather conditions.

Incubation does not begin until the clutch is complete to ensure that the eggs will hatch within a few hours of each other, giving each chick an equal opportunity. Both the male and female birds take their share of the incubation duties, with each bird spending about one and a half hours underground whilst the other is fishing nearby. The incubating Kingfisher waits patiently in the gloom of the chamber, spending most of the time looking down the tunnel and occasionally carefully turning the eggs. The incubation period lasts for nineteen or twenty days and is the part of the breeding season when the Kingfishers are least active.

CHICK DEVELOPMENT

To an observer outside, the first indication that the chicks have hatched is the sight of a parent bird carrying an egg shell away from the nest or returning to the chamber with a tiny fish in its beak. Beneath the ground the little chicks appear weak and helpless, leaning against

12. A Kingfisher first displays aggression to its adversary in an upright posture.

13. The black feet show this bird to be a juvenile; it has caught a huge meal which it will swallow whole.

14. *In courtship the male displays a very upright and angular posture.*

15. *Courtship feeding helps to build a bond between the pair. The lower red mandible of the female can be clearly seen in this photograph.*

each other for warmth and support. They are completely naked and pink, except for a bluish tinge around the tightly sealed eyes. At this stage they are brooded by a parent bird almost constantly. While one adult is brooding the young, the other is fishing. On its return to the nest, with a tiny fish in its beak, the Kingfisher will call to its mate once or twice. The brooding bird will respond by leaving the chicks and moving down and out of the tunnel. The arriving Kingfisher will then feed the fish to a youngster before manoeuvring to the back of the chamber. Settling over the brood, the Kingfisher awaits the return of its mate, when the exchange takes place again.

It is important that the Kingfisher catches small fish for its offspring at this early stage because the fish are always swallowed whole. The Kingfisher does not have the ability to break up fish either for itself or for its young. Sometimes a chick may have difficulty swallowing the food and, although the head of the fish is well swallowed, the tail remains hanging out of its beak for as long as twenty minutes. The chick sits quite still, with its head straining upwards, looking as if it is going to choke to death. Eventually it will gulp the rest of the fish down and settle to rest. Within only a few days each youngster will be eating in the region of fourteen or fifteen fish per day.

At about twelve days old the young Kingfishers' eyes begin to open. They have a more Kingfisher-like appearance as the blue feathers begin to pierce through the skin. Each feather is covered in its own protective sheath to prevent it being abraded as it is rubbed against the rough chamber wall. The chicks are much stronger and no longer need brooding, except at night. As the six or seven youngsters grow they begin to fill the chamber.

The constant calls of the chicks beneath the ground can be heard at the end of the tunnel. Although it is probably only one or two birds calling at any one time, the constant 'churring' sound gives the impression that all the chicks are calling at once. After seventeen days they have the appearance of a Kingfisher wearing a spiky jacket. In shape they are similar to the adults and every feather is

now apparent although they are covered in the protective sheaths. They look rather appealing and comical.

As the youngsters continue to grow rapidly the adults fulfil their demanding calls with a steady supply of fish. The fish are much larger now and a full-grown minnow is about the ideal size. A fish brought up the tunnel and into the chamber is thrust forwards towards the brood. It is then grabbed by the most demanding youngster and as the adult reverses down the tunnel the chick swallows the fish. If its appetite is satisfied, it will push its way to the back of the chamber to rest and allow the other birds to take the front position, facing down the tunnel.

The chamber is kept reasonably clean because of the youngsters habit of ejecting excreta down the tunnel. The tunnel, however, becomes quite filthy and has a strong, sickly, fishy smell. On leaving the tunnel the adults find it necessary to 'plunge bath' into the water once or twice to rid themselves of any excreta sticking to their feathers.

During the last few days in the nest the sheaths covering the feathers split open at the tip. A great deal of nibbling and preening takes place in the overcrowded chamber, until the fully formed feathers are revealed. Now the chamber floor is not only littered with fish bones from regurgitated pellets but is also covered with discarded sheaths. Wing exercising is important to the young Kingfishers at this stage but in the overcrowded nest there is very little room.

FLEDGING

On about the twenty-fourth or twenty-fifth day of life the juvenile birds will make their way down the tunnel and fly. In extreme situations the young may fledge a day earlier but in seasons when fishing is very difficult they may take a few extra days. The young birds are not encouraged out of the nest by the adults, who neither starve them out nor bait them out with food.

Juvenile Kingfishers look very similar to their parents. They are a little smaller and the chestnut/orange breasts have a rather browner appearance. The beak is a little shorter and stockier and each mandible has a white tip. The feet of juvenile birds are quite black when they first leave the nest. It is therefore possible to identify juvenile birds by the white tip on the beak and the black feet. As the bird matures, over a period of several months, the white tip fades away and the feet gradually change from black to red. The sex of the Kingfisher is indistinguishable as a fledgling and it is probably two, or even three, months before the lower mandible of the female begins to show the red area developing from the base.

The juvenile Kingfishers spend the first day or two out of the nest staring at the sky. They rely on their parents to feed them, attracting their attention with a call that is only used at this period of their life. It is a short, sharp, 'chip-chip' sound, repeated two or three times in succession. The brood makes no attempt to remain together and a row of fledglings lined up to be fed by the parent birds is a most unusual sight. The youngsters weakly fly to a variety of trees and shrubs along the river bank and the adults search them out over several hundred yards of river. Juveniles are not taught to catch fish by their parents; in fact many young Kingfishers will be chased out of the adults' territory never having seen a fish caught. Only three or four days after the youngsters fledge the parents will suddenly turn aggressive towards their offspring, violently chasing them away from the territory because the adult birds will almost certainly attempt a second brood. On rare occasions it is possible that a third brood may be raised, especially if some mishap occurred to one of the earlier broods.

The young birds are completely alone as they establish their own territory and learn to catch fish; it is a very difficult time and many do not survive. Eventually hunger will force them to dive into the water to try to catch a fish, but because of their inexperience the success rate is not very high. It is a great help if the river is very shallow when they are trying to catch fish for the first time. Shoals of small fish swarm in the warm shallow areas and are much easier to catch than fish in deeper water.

Many juvenile birds chased from their parents' home range will inadvertently arrive in another Kingfisher's territory. Such a newcomer will immediately be chased from the area and so the juvenile learns to be cunning and arrive at a new location in silence. It will then have the opportunity to catch a few fish before being disturbed by the occupier of the territory. If left undisturbed, the youngster will call quietly, once or twice and as long as it is left untroubled, its confidence builds up until eventually it flies up and down the water calling loudly and defiantly, declaring ownership of the territory.

MORTALITY

With the potential of one, two or even three broods of youngsters being raised each year, and six or seven fledglings leaving the nest from each brood, it may seem strange that the Kingfisher is not a more common sight on rivers and streams. Clearly there is heavy mortality amongst Kingfishers in most years, keeping the population in check.

Within only two months of leaving the nest over half of the juveniles will have died. By their first breeding season, when they will be one year old, only one quarter of them will have survived to breed. As we have seen, the parents chase away the young birds often before they have learned to fish. Forced by hunger, the inexperienced bird may make several attempts to dive for a fish without any success. Plenty of practice is needed before the technique of getting in and out of the water without getting too wet is mastered. Each time the youngster dives it becomes more tired and more waterlogged and some juveniles drown. Others may become so wet that they are unable to dry their plumage before the sun sets and so they face the cold night in a wet, tired and hungry condition.

In general the Kingfisher does not suffer heavily from predation. Domestic cats are able to catch a few each year and Sparrowhawks are also predators. It has been suggested that the flesh of the Kingfisher is distasteful and that this is indicated to predators by its colour. However, Kingfishers are known to have been taken by Sparrowhawks because their remains have been found in their

16. *The female Kingfisher incubates the eggs in the secrecy and security of the nest chamber.*

17. *At only a day or two old the chicks are featherless and blind; they are brooded almost constantly by an adult at this stage.*

18. *Every feather of this chick is covered in a sheath to protect it from abrasion while underground.*

19. *As an adult offers a fish to the hungry brood the nearest youngster grabs it with great enthusiasm.*

nests. Man also used to be a common predator, catching Kingfishers with traps for their beautiful feathers, which were then used for trout fishing flies and were supposed to be irresistible bait to fish. Kingfisher feathers have also been credited with a variety of magical powers, including the power to prevent lightning striking one who wears them.

However, Kingfishers suffer most from the weather. A very high proportion of adult bird deaths in Britain can be attributed to winter cold or freezing conditions. Whenever the Kingfisher wants a meal it has to dive into the icy water and if the 'larder' of fish is locked away beneath a layer of ice many birds will die. Other Kingfishers will move down river and this will, no doubt, cause territorial disputes as they make their way towards the harbours and estuaries where the brackish water is less likely to freeze.

On some rivers flooding is also a significant problem. If floods take place during the breeding season many eggs may be lost or chicks drowned in their nests. However, this does not often occur as floods more usually happen during the non-breeding months. Nevertheless, during periods of heavy flooding the familiar environment of the river is completely altered and Kingfishers lose track of their territory or need to move to a new area to find easier fishing. Once again territorial disputes occur, energy is wasted and time is lost as the Kingfishers contest a suitable fishing area.

An adult bird may live long enough to breed for three or four seasons and in that time will produce many youngsters. Although the weather may drastically reduce Kingfisher numbers the species is still resilient. Given the opportunity, they are able to increase rapidly during more favourable seasons.

20. *A goldfish pond which is regularly visited by a Kingfisher. A branch has been placed over the pond as a suitable perch.*

21. *The author arranging a branch in front of a hide at a Kingfisher's favourite fishing location.*

Watching Kingfishers

Everyone who enjoys natural history gets a special thrill from the sight of a Kingfisher. With such bright and distinctive plumage it is difficult to imagine how a Kingfisher on a local lake or stream could be overlooked. However, the Kingfisher is a notoriously difficult bird to find and even harder to observe at close quarters. There are always the exceptions and many anglers tell of the Kingfishers which have perched on their fishing rods. A few individuals may become accustomed to the presence of people or traffic, but in general it remains a frustrating bird to observe.

The sight of a Kingfisher is usually described as 'a flash of blue disappearing up river'. This describes something of the Kingfisher's character, because having observed a human it takes alarm sooner than most birds of a similar size. Once disturbed many other species of comparable size merely fly a few yards away into the next bush. It is easy to watch these birds with binoculars but the Kingfisher always seems to fly right away, at least around the bend of the stream and out of sight.

The best approach to Kingfisher watching is to understand the bird's habits and to become familiar with its distinctive call. Recognising its piercing whistle enables the observer to anticipate the arrival of a Kingfisher. Commonly the call is used in flight as the bird moves from one part of its territory to another. On hearing the call it is much more profitable simply to sit and wait for five or ten minutes than to go in search of the bird. In this way a quiet and still observer is more likely to enjoy a prolonged view of the subject than merely the familiar flash of blue.

Kingfishers have favourite fishing spots although these may change from time to time as the condition of the river changes, resulting in moving shoals of small fish. It is easier for a human observer to find fish swarming in shallow water than it is to find a Kingfisher. Having gained a little knowledge that a bird is on a particular stretch of river (by hearsay, by a fleeting glimpse or sound) then it is very worthwhile to wait for its arrival. Clearly it helps to be hidden from view and binoculars can be used from a nearby bush.

Very close observation is possible from a simply constructed hide. Hides should be made from light-proof material that will not flap, and provided the eye slots for observation are narrow the Kingfisher will not be disturbed by the observer's movements. It is important that the position or construction of the hide does not disturb either the Kingfisher or other wildlife in the area. Enthusiasts may even contrive a method of keeping a constant shoal of minnows close to a hide, which was how the author's seven years of Kingfisher observation was achieved. It must be pointed out, however, that if this idea is adopted the observer has a moral obligation to continue the supply of food as long as the Kingfisher relies upon it and that this is not easy as the season changes from autumn to winter.

In general, observation is easier and more rewarding during the summer months when the birds are most active, supplying the demands of their youngsters. Also at this time of year the juvenile birds may be a little more confiding, as they search for their own territories. Care must be taken during the breeding season not to disturb the birds' activities and it is illegal to erect a hide near a nest site without a permit from the Nature Conservancy Council.

It is not an easy bird to observe but the effort is very worthwhile and it was once suggested that 'only the righteous ever see the Kingfisher'.

FURTHER READING

Boag, David. *The Kingfisher.* Blandford Press, 1982.
Eastman, Rosemary. *The Kingfisher.* Collins, 1969.
Lovegrove, R., and Snow, P. *River Birds.* Columbus Books, 1984.
Morgan, R., and Glue, D. 'Breeding Mortality and Movement of Kingfishers'. *Bird Study,* 1976.
Sharrock, S. T. R. *The Atlas of Breeding Birds in Britain and Ireland.* British Trust for Ornithology, 1970.

NATIONAL SOCIETIES

British Trust for Ornithology, Beech Grove, Tring, Hertfordshire HP23 5NR.
Royal Society for Nature Conservation, The Green, Nettleham, Lincoln LN2 2NR.
Royal Society for the Protection of Birds, The Lodge, Sandy, Bedfordshire SG19 2DL.

ACKNOWLEDGEMENTS

All photographs are by the author except for 4, 10 and 11, which are by Mike Mockler.